What a blessing it was  1
book that provides a beaut
developing a true relationsh
lenge outlined in this book h
many others. The spiritual struggle is real. This 40-Day Challenge truly will Ignite Your Soul!

Jason Nowell
President Ashton Gray

I met Ross at a time in my life when my husband and I were
clinging to the Lord in grief after the death of our son. For the
service, I had written out and shared my prayer for our heartbro-
ken family. In that moment, I didn't fully understand the impact
it would have on me spiritually and how much it would comfort
me until far later. Through friendship and heartfelt coaching,
Ross not only helped to reignite my soul, but consistently reminded me to trust God in all things, both personally and pro-
fessionally; to go to Him in prayer for what we need and to also
thank Him for what He has already done in our lives. The experiences and advice Ross shares in this beautiful book resonate
because so many of us have been through trials and struggles
that challenge our faith. Written with openness and honesty, it
is a must-read for anyone who wants to draw nearer to the Lord
and begin to recognize His powerful healing and glory.

Karla Graham
Director, Economic & Workforce Development
Metro Technology Centers

"Heaven and earth will disappear, but my words will never disappear." Matthew 24:35

Miracles truly happen when we combine the Word of God and His promises into our prayer life. The fact that I am writing this recommendation for Fuel to Ignite Your Soul is one of those miracles. My wife had prayed for almost 2 years for God to bring godly mentors around me, and it started with a 40-day devotion that was gifted to her by a friend called Draw the Circle by Mark Batterson. She started praying and circling her prayers daily. In one of the chapters, Mark spoke of a businessman from Oklahoma that had shared the Gospel in his office with over 3,000 new clients. This sparked my wife's curiosity and gave her courage to look up Ross and connect with him through LinkedIn. Shortly after their first conversation over the phone, the Hill family invited us to their home in Oklahoma.

In a normal world, a Lebanese-born entrepreneur living in Massachusetts would have never met Ross or his beautiful wife, RJ, but God had a different plan. God makes the impossible possible, is a friend to the needy, and He makes miracles happen. This is how I feel about Ross's book. It is the plan that can align our words with God's Word and transform prayers into miracles! My relationship with Ross came about by prayer. It was God's plans aligned with my wife's prayers that led to this most amazing friendship…a divine connection that only God could orchestrate.

I highly recommend this book and believe that when you read it and apply a daily practice of reading God's Word and journaling your prayers, you will encounter God in the most miraculous and supernatural way. I know and believe it because the fact that I am writing this recommendation is a testimony of what Ross is teaching through this 40-Day Challenge.

Charbel H. Najem
Co-founder Cedarwood Realty Group. Inc

Rarely will you meet a person who has a true passion to encourage others. Ross Alan Hill is one of those people. The first time I met Ross he shared his 40-Day Challenge with me. Ross not only shared the concept, but he also showed me dozens of prayer journals which represented decades of life as he prayed for his family and friends. Ross's book is a must read for anyone wanting to deepen their prayer life.

Keven Baker
Senior Pastor
Martha Road Baptist Church

FUEL TO IGNITE
YOUR SOUL
THE 40-DAY CHALLENGE

ROSS ALAN HILL
FOREWORD BY MARK BATTERSON

Contents

A Word from the Author | Guarantee ix

Foreword | Mark Batterson xiii

Dedication xv

SECTION 1 | THE PROBLEM

Introduction | Missing My Love 3

Chapter 1 | My Spiritual Life Was Nonexistent..................... 7

Chapter 2 | My Inability to Pray Was Systemic 15

Chapter 3 | The Root Cause, My Empty Spiritual Life 21

SECTION 2 | THE PRESCRIPTION

Chapter 4 | The 40-Day Challenge 27

Chapter 5 | Pick A Time.................................. 31

Chapter 6 | Pick A Place 37

Chapter 7 | A Chapter A Day 43

Chapter 8 | Pray Using a Prayer Journal.................... 53

Chapter 9 | Top 10 Surprises of Using a Prayer Journal 61

Chapter 10 | His Presence 67

Chapter 11 | Hope and Encouragement............................. 71

Chapter 12 | David's Prayer Journal 75

SECTION 3 | THE PREPARATION

Chapter 13 | Toolbox.. 83
Epilogue 85
Acknowledgments 87
About the Author 89
Notes 90

Why did I write this book?

Please allow me to frame my personal situation for you starting back in the early 1990's. I had some huge problems in my spiritual life which held me back from a deep personal relationship with Jesus. It kept me from being all God expected me to be. I was not being a light to the world.

As a follower of Jesus, we are to live like Jesus. We are to light the way for others to come to know Jesus: to live in such a way people would ask why we act like we do and why we are filled with joy and love. We are to live in such a way our life reflects Jesus. Every believer is called to make disciples and there is no better way to do so than to reflect Jesus in the way we live.

I was not accomplishing my purpose on earth, nor was I living a life filled with joy. I carelessly thought I was the only one. No one had ever told me they were having issues in their spiritual life. I heard people talk about their spiritual life with great passion. I wondered what was wrong with me. I was in a rough spot. I kept all of this a secret because I was embarrassed and ashamed. At times, my problems were so acute they foolishly made me doubt my salvation. Thankfully, I figured out a partial solution back in the mid-1990's when I saw a book title that caught my attention. It was titled *Too Busy Not to Pray*. When I saw the book and read the title, I instantly picked it up. I could relate to the title. Then, I saw it was written by a very famous pastor, and so I bought it. The book helped me get my spiritual life moving in the right direction. Years later, another book, *The Circle Maker*, broadened my understanding and energized my spiritual life a great deal. The author, Pastor Mark Batterson, became a friend who personally coached me in prayer and the use of a prayer journal. Then, with some good old-fashioned effort and resolve, along with the Holy Spirit, his coaching helped me overcome my weaknesses. It was a great day when my problems were resolved!

My spiritual life strengthened; and after some time had passed, I discovered I was not alone. Many, if not most, Christians suffer in silence from the same problems that had plagued my own Spiritual life. Slowly, I began sharing how I solved my problems with friends. It worked! Then, I shared it with some employees and had the same positive results. Finally, one of my clients asked for help, and it was successful for them, too! Around the same time, I was asked to speak to complete strangers about my method, which I was a little hesitant to do. These people were also able to overcome their issues. Joy filled my soul!

Since then, many people have asked, "Ross, there are millions who need help fixing their spiritual life. Why not write a book about how you solved your spiritual relationship problems?" These comments caused me to reflect on their idea. Certainly, a couple of books and a friend had helped to set my spiritual life on fire. With so many people encouraging me to share my experience, I was motivated to write this book to help others build a heartfelt relationship with Jesus, just like I had done.

I know the pain of not knowing how to build a real relationship with Jesus. I lived it for nearly 30 years. The negative emotions were real, but I learned how to solve my problems. So, I thought, why not share my method with everyone?

I started writing this book in 2015. I coined my method *The 40-Day Challenge*, because it only takes 40 days to form a lifelong habit providing the *"FUEL to Ignite Your Soul" for the rest of your life*. This method has been successfully tested and tried by countless men and women and even a 7 year old named Eli. I say with confidence: **I will refund your money for the purchase price of this book if it does not significantly improve your relationship with Jesus.**

GUARANTEE*

The steps to receive a refund of the purchase price of this book are as follows:

A. Read this book (estimated 2 hours).
B. Complete *"The 40-Day Challenge"* (estimate 40 hours), utilizing all methods described. If, when you are finished, if you do not find your spiritual life has been transformed, simply:
  1. Send your receipt of purchase and this book
  2. Include a request for a refund
  3. Mail to: rah360 LLC, PO Box 30900, Edmond, OK 73003
  4. Be sure to include a return address.

We will refund your money within 30 days of receiving these items.

---

*This personal guarantee is limited to a maximum of $20.00 and must be requested within one year of the date of purchase on the receipt.

Foreword

By Mark Batterson

The first time I met Ross Hill, he showed up wearing shoes that said *Chase the Lion*. Needless to say, I liked him immediately! Ross is definitely a lion chaser! I felt like I had found a kindred spirit. The more I got to know Ross, the more I appreciated his business mind and ministry heart. It's a combination that is more critical than ever.

If I had to describe Ross in a single phrase, it might be *big-hearted*. He has big faith, big compassion, and big dreams. But it's his big heart for others, myself included, that I admire most. Ross is one of those rare people that is all about everyone else. As you'll discover in the pages that follow, it wasn't always that way.

Truth be told, all of us start out selfish. It's hard not to when the world revolves around you. At some point, we need to discover that we don't keep the planets in orbit. The sooner the better! That can be painful at first, but it's absolutely liberating. Why? Because you can stop playing God, which is awfully exhausting.

Everybody needs somebody in life who stretches their faith. Ross is one of those people in my life. Before releasing *The Circle Maker*, Ross circled a number and texted it to me. It was the number of copies he believed that book would sell. Let's just say that it was a few million more than my wildest dreams. A decade later, God has answered that circled prayer, plus some.

I share that to share this: let this book stretch your faith. If you feel absolutely ordinary, you'll discover that you aren't alone. If your dreams seem impossible, welcome to the club. The good news? There is a God whose power is made perfect in our weakness! I pray that the genuine humility and practical advice you find in the pages that follow will help you take the next step in your Spiritual journey!

Dedication

This book is dedicated to my wife, Raynell (R.J.), who, more than anyone on earth, has believed in me and challenged me to be a man of God. She reminds me, repeatedly, it is not about me. It is about serving others. She reminds me to love like Jesus. To live like Jesus. To respond to hate, unkindness, or selfishness like Jesus would. She challenges me to step up and live my faith. She reminds me to not worry about what others think or say but, instead, to just live out my calling and my anointing.

She wholeheartedly believed God would provide our place of ministry. On January 15, 2020, we closed on "Hidden Treasure," an eight acre spot hidden in the middle of Edmond, Oklahoma. It is surrounded by water on three sides and has over 100 trees, mostly mighty oaks. All kinds of wildlife lives on this beautiful land. Many people instinctively call it a *"hidden treasure"* without knowing it is the name we chose for this gift from God. Like the parable in the Book of Matthew 13:44, we sold everything we had to buy it and turn it into a place of ministry to pastors. R.J. was 100% on-board and had absolutely no reservations.

When I grow weak, she is strong and encouraging. R.J. reminds me to stay humble. She completes me in every way. She is a Proverbs 31 woman. She is my eternal partner in our ministry. She knows the value of *The 40-Day Challenge,* for it dramatically changed her relationship with Jesus, as well.

R.J., thank you for encouraging me to finish this book and for unselfishly giving me the time and space to do so.

I love you with all of my heart!

Ross aka your boyfried

SECTION ONE

THE PROBLEM

Introduction

MISSING MY LOVE

My wife, R.J., and I were blessed with our 17th grandchild in August of 2018. R.J. was out-of-town helping our daughter-in-law learn the daunting tasks involved in caring for her first baby. In August and September, she made several trips to Kansas City to lend a hand. On one trip, R.J. was gone for eleven days, and I really missed her. It was hard for me to not hear her laugh, see her smile, and hold her hand. Mealtimes and night times were especially lonely. The positive side of it all was it reminded me how much I love her and how terrible it would be to go through life without her. Lord, may it never be!

A few weeks later, I had minor surgery and was laid up for about a week. I was on pain meds for three or four days, so I missed spending time with the Lord. I felt like I did when I missed R.J. while she was in Kansas City.

FALLING IN LOVE WITH JESUS

This was the first time I could remember deeply missing

my daily time with The Lord. It registered with me because my feelings were the same intense yearning I felt missing my wife while she was away. *How cool is that?* I thought. I truly missed spending time with The Lord. I could not *ever* remember missing Him with such passion.

In previous times, I would feel guilt about not reading the Bible and praying, but I could *not* remember the strong emotional longing for time with The Lord. This made me stop in my tracks. It grabbed my attention. It was an amazing moment in my life.

It was an important breakthrough for me. As I reflected on it, all kinds of questions ran through my mind.

- What just happened?
- What happened in my life that caused me to miss The Lord?
- When did I fall in love with The Lord?
- Why was I so surprised?
- Do others feel the same way too?
- I have not heard anyone speak about it. Why?

I was fascinated, but more importantly, God used it to help motivate me to finish this book. You see, I had started writing the book but never seemed to be able to finish it. My writing seemed mechanical, like a machine or a robot. What I wrote was boring. It lacked emotion. It was formula driven instead of a story about my journey and how my life had turned around because I found a way to have a personal relationship with The Lord. God used this recent experience to motivate me to write and re-write and re-write it again until I got it right. What you are about to read is the catalyst for my spiritual life. It changed me for the good; and if you apply the contents and complete *The 40-Day Challenge*, I believe God will use it as a game-changer for your spiritual life for eternity too. I am completely confident of this.

There is simply no power, no knowledge, no university degree, no training class, no amount of personal effort, no work ethic, no job, no profession, no amount of money or fame that can compensate you sufficiently for the absence of a personal relationship with Jesus built not just on loving Jesus, but rather *being in love with Jesus*. It is the **Fuel to Ignite Your Soul.**

CHAPTER I

My Spiritual Life was Nonexistent

HAVE YOU EVER...

Do you wonder, where is God?

Have you ever questioned if you are really saved?

Have you ever thought, maybe I did not say the right words, or maybe my baptism was done wrong?

Have you ever felt like you must have messed up and The Lord has left you in the dust?

Have you ever thought there must be more to being a Christian?

Have you ever wondered why some people seem to know God better than you do?

Have you ever questioned, where is His power?

Have you ever asked, why don't I hear the voice of God?

Have you ever felt like you are just going through the motions?

Have you ever wondered why there does not seem to be any tangible difference between most people who say they are Christians and the rest of the people of the world?

I HAVE, AND MUCH MORE!

That was me! Those were my thoughts, doubts and questions. I can still remember the heavy weight and burden these placed on my heart. If similar thoughts have crossed your mind, keep reading. This book was written for *you*.

BACKSTORY

I had become a follower of Jesus between my junior and senior years in high school at the First Christian Church in Springfield, Ohio. A group, *Come Alive Singers,* from Cincinnati Bible Seminary were holding a youth revival, and Roy Mays, III was a student preacher who did most of the speaking over the weekend. Professor Tom Friskney preached on Friday night, August 3, 1970. At the conclusion of his message, I stepped out of the pew and walked down the aisle to accept Jesus as my Savior. I was baptized that very night. In order to baptize me, they had to take up part of the flooring on the platform in the church as the baptistry was under the platform.

The minister of the church, John Wilson, took an immediate liking to me, recognizing my potential. He taught me how to write a portion of a sermon and had me preach on Sunday night several times during my senior year of high school. He literally forced the hand of the Cincinnati Bible Seminary to accept me as a student. I officially majored in English Bible, (no Greek or Hebrew classes) with a minor in Ministry. In practice, I majored in *sleeping*, and minored in *skipping* the maximum number of classes allowed to still earn credit for the class. I did exceptionally well in the *sleeping* and *skipping* degree programs (A+) and managed to stay on probation all four years in the English Bible and Ministry degree programs.

I say, my pastor "forced" the college because that is exactly what he did! He would not take "no" from the registrar at the college. I was finally accepted into school on an exception basis. Without John Wilson insisting I be allowed to enroll, it would never have happened. I found out later, my pastor had been on the board of trustees for decades. His influence at the school was impressive and he used his influence to help me.

As a leader, I know the power of influence, and I highly value it. Most of the leaders I know feel the same way. Leaders, including myself, do not typically take high risks with their influence as it can be lost if not used wisely. Understanding this *today* helps me realize *now* how much my pastor loved me and believed in me. He had only known me on a limited basis for a short period of time. The man did not know my parents. He knew me as the boyfriend of one of the teenagers who went to his church. Yet, with little direct knowledge in the span of just over one year, he elected to spend a great deal of his *"influence currency"* on my behalf.

The Lord had, somehow, given me favor with my pastor, so he risked his influence and insisted the school admit me.

As I write these words tonight, I wonder *why* had he taken such a risk? It literally causes a lump in my throat and brings tears to my eyes to realize my minister believed in me far more than I believed in myself. Foolishly, and regretfully, I had never shown him the proper gratitude for his efforts on my behalf. Honestly, as I write these words, the significance of his remarkable deed is just now being fully realized by me. *God used John Wilson to dramatically change the trajectory of my life.* I have praised God for John Wilson in the past, but never like I am at this very moment.

At the time, I was too young and immature to understand what Pastor Wilson was doing for me. I only hope his family knows the impact he had on me, and somehow he knows from heaven how thankful I am that he was willing to risk his influence to help me.

John Wilson, Mighty Man of God, Thank YOU!

TREATED LIKE I WAS SPECIAL

As a young adult with a Bible college education, I was always asked to teach or lead at church. As a result, I have done everything you can possibly think of in a church. The following is a partial list:

- Nursery
- Junior church
- Middle AND senior high Sunday school teacher
- Youth group leader
- Taught adult Sunday school classes
- Taught senior adults
- Filled in for the pastor and preached on occasion
- Chairman of the Board for my church
- I tithed
- I passed communion
- I took up the offerings
- I even ran the sound system for the church at times!

To most people, I looked like a good, strong, committed Christian man. I prayed in church for the offering or communion and whenever called upon at other times.

LIVING A SECRET

I did not have a personal walk with Jesus. I NEVER read the Bible except on rare occasions or to teach a class or preach a sermon. If it were not for the fact that I kept it in the same drawer, I would never have been able to find it. I did not know how to pronounce many of the words in it, and it bored me. I did not believe it had any real value. I sure did not want to read it every day.

I could not finish my own personal prayers. You know, when you are all alone, trying to talk to The Lord, I just could not do it. Every time I prayed, my mind drifted off to the golf course or to a meeting or television show—anything and anywhere but on Holy things. This happened all the time!

My personal prayer time was so bad that when I had trouble falling asleep, I would just start praying and I would go to sleep almost instantly. Some people drink warm milk to fall asleep, others will turn on the television or music, some count sheep, and some take a pill. Not me. I would just roll over and begin praying and the next thing I know my alarm was going off the next morning. For me, prayer was the perfect cure for insomnia.

It was true, and even as I write these words in 2020, it is hard to admit publicly I had such a poor spiritual life.

It was sad.

I was sad.

FELT LIKE A FAILURE

All of this was happening in total silence. No one knew the pain I was feeling. I wanted to talk to someone, but who? I was the Chairman of the Board of my church. Who was I going to talk to? I did not have a mentor/coach at the time. I had some close friends, but I was too embarrassed to tell them what was going on. My pride was too big! It got so bad, I started questioning my own salvation. I was dying on the inside and had convinced myself I could not share my problem with anyone. I was so ashamed and I believed no one would understand. As a result, I felt all alone and isolated. I felt like I had failed God and, worse, that God had deserted me. Have you ever felt this way? Feelings can be misleading. The truth is, God never leaves us. We are His children, and He loves us with an everlasting love. We might choose to leave Him, but He never leaves us.

I STOPPED

So I would not feel so defeated, I stopped praying; and even though I did not read the Bible much to begin with, I stopped reading it entirely. Stopping both was not a big deal, I reasoned in my mind. At least this way, I wouldn't be reminded about my hollow Christian life. I went to church and I tithed, so I had that going for me. I tried to lay low and do nothing except when called upon in public. I would have been absolutely humiliated if anyone found out about my weak spiritual life.

I bought some books on prayer; but to be honest with you, they bored me to tears. I needed something down to earth and practical, not some high and mighty book full of lofty prayer instructions I barely understood, written by someone light years ahead of me, spiritually speaking. I needed a book that was rational, sensible, and easy to read. I never found one.

Satan was winning and I was losing. I was getting weaker and weaker and the distance between me and Jesus was becoming as vast as the 60-mile wide Great Rift Valley in East Africa!

BREAKTHROUGH

As I mentioned earlier, in the early 1990's, things started to change. I was in a bookstore when I stumbled onto a book written by the pastor of one of America's largest churches. He confessed consistently experiencing the same problems I was having in my prayer life.

I could hardly believe what I was reading. I thought, *"If one of the most successful pastors in America has the same problem, there might be hope for me!"* So, I kept reading.

As I read, the pastor went on to explain how he had solved his prayer problems. He wrote his prayers out word for word on a yellow pad.

I was soaking in the bathtub when I read those words. I got out of the tub, wrapped a towel around myself and went to retrieve a yellow pad out of my briefcase. Pen and pad in hand,

I climbed back into the tub, and started writing out my prayers word for word.

It changed my life!

———————————

"Your prayer life and the trajectory of your spiritual life are explicitly linked together."

— Ross Alan Hill

———————————

CHAPTER 2

The Inability to Pray was Systemic

SELDOM READ THE BIBLE

My inability to pray was systemic to larger problems. I never read the Bible except to prepare to preach a message, teach a Sunday school lesson, or lead a youth group meeting. I certainly did not know how to pronounce a bunch of the words (in fact, at age 68, I am still working on that one) nor did I know the order of the books of the Bible or a hundred other details. While I had studied most of the books of the Bible in college, I did not know them well. Remember, I skipped class a lot and stayed on probation my entire four years in college.

Because I did not become a Christian until age 17, I never learned the great stories of the Bible as a child. Every once in a while, however, I found verses and stories in the Bible with which I identified. A passage from the Book of Jeremiah resonated in my soul the first time I read it.

It was as though God wrote those words to me, personally. Those words still have a significant impact on my life. If you ever happen to be in the audience when I am preparing to speak, watch closely. Right before I begin, you will see I am reading from the Bible. I am reading those verses. They have become my prayer every time I speak.

Below is this very special passage of Scripture.

The Lord gave me this message: "I knew you before I formed you in your mother's womb. Before you were born I set you apart and appointed you as my prophet to the nations."

"O Sovereign Lord," I said, "I can't speak for you! I'm too young!"

The Lord replied, "Don't say, 'I'm too young,' for you must go wherever I send you and say whatever I tell you. And don't be afraid of the people, for I will be with you and will protect you. I, the Lord have spoken!"

Then the Lord reached out and touched my mouth and said, "Look, I have put my words in your mouth! Today I appoint you to stand up against nations and kingdoms. Some you must uproot and tear down, destroy and overthrow. Others you must build up and plant."
—Jeremiah 1:4–10

SCRIPTURE IMPACTED MY LIFE

The impact made on my life by the Book of Jeremiah was so significant that I named my first son Jeremy, after Jeremiah. Like the Book of Jeremiah, Jeremy has had a significant impact on my life and my experience as a parent.

I liked the story of the twelve spies and the vision to build and attempt the impossible as told in the Book of Numbers. So, I named my second son after Caleb. I wanted him to be a loyal friend, loyal to the call of God to do what is right, and loyal to the truth. I wanted him to know that "with God, all things are possible." My son, Caleb, has spent his life attempting the impossible.

The story of the Valley of Dry Bones from the Book of Ezekiel so healed my brokenness and gave me such hope that I named my third son Ezekiel. In his life, he has seen a lot of brokenness, but he knows God faithfully heals the brokenhearted.

For those reasons, and maybe more, some concluded that I must have been a devoted Christian. They were wrong. I was a Christian in name only. I was totally empty on the inside.

**"You must love the Lord your God with all your heart,
all your soul, all your strength, and all your mind."**

— Luke 10:27

This means *ALL* of your **heart, soul, strength,** and **mind**.

Knowing God involves having a personal relationship with Him. It is like loving your spouse or kids. If you do not talk, laugh, and listen to your spouse or your children, you are not going to have a strong relationship. The words of Jesus in response to a question about the most important commandment in the law of Moses—*"Jesus replied, 'You must love the Lord your God with all your heart, all your soul, and all your mind.' This is the first and greatest commandment. A second is equally important: 'Love your neighbor as yourself.' The entire law and all the demands of the prophets are based upon these two commandments."* — Matthew 22:37–40

The Greatest Commandment is direct and directional. Yet, unfortunately, they are too often ignored by billions of people.

It is difficult to keep the greatest commandment if you do not pray and do not read the Bible. These are our *primary* relational touch points with Jesus. Without them, how can you say you love Him?

God mostly teaches and speaks through His Word. If we

don't read His Word, it is hard to hear Him, much less know His voice. He told us to hide the Word in our hearts. Again, it is impossible to hide it in your heart if you do not read His Word! It is also difficult to hide them in your heart if you do not memorize them or pray them.

There is no shortcut to any close, deep, loving relationship. It takes time and effort. But The Lord gives us a great promise if we pursue him.

> "When you seek me in prayer and worship,
> you will find me available to you.
> *If you seek me with all your heart and soul,*
> *I will make myself available to you," says the Lord.*
>
> — Jeremiah 29:13–14 (NET)

PLEASE, DO NOT FEEL GUILTY

Please, do not feel guilty. That is not my purpose nor my goal. I felt the sting of guilt for years, and I would never intentionally try to spread those feelings to others. Instead, my goal is the exact opposite. I want to encourage you by allowing you to see how empty I used to be and to help you realize it does not have to be that way. Simply said, it takes effort to keep a solid relationship with your family and friends. It takes the same effort, and maybe a little more, to have a solid relationship with Jesus. My hope is you will see me as someone who was adrift yet found his way. Believe His promise, with Him you can do this.

Maybe you are wondering, can it really happen for me? Could my life be different? Can I know Jesus? How? What do I need to do? God showed me the way through a couple of books. I have spent years writing this book just for you. My goal is to give you hope and encouragement by sharing with you how empty I was, how I walked the same path you might be on, and how I found my way to a meaningful relationship with Jesus through seeking Him daily by reading the Bible and through prayer. *You can, too!*

————————————

"I am profitably engaged in reading the Bible.
Take all of this Book that you can by reason
and the balance by faith, and you will live and die a better man.
It is the best Book which God has given to man."

— Abraham Lincoln
16th President of the United States

————————————

CHAPTER 3

The Root Cause, My Empty Spiritual Life

THE PROBLEM WAS ME

I did **not** know Jesus. I did meet Him on August 3, 1970. But I never developed a deep, meaningful relationship with Him. It was no one's fault but my own. I simply did not know how to have a personal relationship with—what seemed to me—an invisible God named Jesus. I could *not* sit down and talk face-to-face with Jesus. I could *not* hug Him or put my arm around His shoulder. I am an includer—the more, the merrier. I am relational, so I enjoy talking to others face-to-face, not on the telephone or on a Zoom or FaceTime call. I need and *want* to meet in person. I like the energy and bonding relationship created by in person meetings.

My friends and grandkids know I like to hug. My grand-daughter, Lauren, wrote in a book, "Papa gives the *BEST* hugs." It brought the biggest smile to my face and was music to my ears. It is part of my love language and it helps me build rela-tionships. How do I hug Jesus? How can I see Jesus to pray to Him? How can I hear Jesus? How do I see His facial expressions when we talk? So, for me, it was true: **I was adrift**.

I needed a road map, something to fuel my relationship with Jesus, but I never found it. Honestly, I had become very frustrated and tired and, basically, living as a shell. However, if I want to be accurate, my attempts were lackluster at best. I had heard about reading and studying the Bible and knew about Bible reading plans. I even took some classes on those topics, but nothing helped. Why? Mostly because I was not willing to pay the price of working hard and building discipline into my life.

I bought lots of books about prayer with subjects like how to pray, intercessory prayer, corporate prayer, listening for God's voice, "believing and it shall be done" kinds of prayers, and about praying Scriptures over your life. To be honest, I do not think I finished any of those books on prayer because they bored me! They were too formal and what they said just did not stick with me. It seemed totally hypothetical and exceedingly difficult for me to comprehend. Many read like a textbook. Maybe I had a mental block?

Soon, I did not have any interest in prayer, nor did I have an interest in reading the Bible. Both seemed very boring to me and had no real value.

I wanted the salvation Jesus offered, but I did not want to spend the time trying to figure out something which seemed so difficult and abstract. I even reasoned, if it was so important to Jesus, He should make the way clear and easy. My attitude was like, *"It is His responsibility to figure it out, NOT mine. After all, He is God, He should know how to make it simple."*

The fact is, He did!

**"You will seek and find me
when you seek me with all your heart."**

— Jeremiah 29:13 (NIV)

In other words, if you want a relationship with Jesus, it requires a lot of effort on your part. It requires us to seek Him with all our heart.

Did you catch the last line? Some have said to me, *"I love Jesus, but I am not **in love** with Jesus."* You see, they realize they want his *presents*; they wanted the trappings He has to offer, but they really do not want Him to have a *presence* in their lives.

It is hard to love your wife or your family if all you do is give them presents as a substitute for your attention. To love your wife or your family, it takes your presence, not just presents. You must spend time with them, doing the things they like to do. It requires your time and attention as well as your empathy, care, concern, and your involvement.

In fact, again, He made it simple. Two more verses sum it up.

"Keep on asking, and you will receive what you ask for.
Keep on seeking, and you will find.
Keep on knocking, *and the door will be opened to you.*
For everyone who asks, receives. Everyone who seeks, finds.
And to everyone who knocks, the door will be opened."
— Matthew 7:7–9

All your heart, soul, strength, and mind.

"Seek the Kingdom of God above all else,
and live righteously, and he will give you everything you need."
— Matthew 6:33

SEEK ME

If you will **seek Jesus,** you will **find** Him. Those are His words, not mine. It is really that simple. It takes work and discipline, but it is not complicated nor is it impossible.

Do you know this truth?

"Blessings live in the land of obedience."

— Ross Alan Hill

Jesus said it this way...

"When you obey my commandments,
You remain in my love,
Just as I obey my Father's Commandments and remain in his love."

— John 15:10

SECTION TWO

THE PRESCRIPTION

CHAPTER 4

The 40-Day Challenge

This is the simple plan I created to help fuel my spiritual life. It is how I have helped thousands of others do the same.

THE IDEA BEHIND THE NAME

As I began sharing my journey with others and what I learned about having a relationship with Jesus, I gave my system a name: *The 40-Day Challenge,* the sub title to this book. The idea behind the name was scripturally based.

There are numerous references to the number 40 in the Scriptures. One reference is how Jesus spent 40 days in the desert, fasting and praying and being tempted in numerous ways by Satan. The 40 days in the desert was a strenuous challenge for Jesus; yet He overcame all the temptations with strength and courage, through prayer and fasting. It seemed to me a great theme for what I was doing and wanted to teach others to do. I am not suggesting you spend 40 days in the desert, but I do want you to spend 40 days with The Lord, getting to know Him on a personal basis. It is challenging on its own merit, but it is a much more pleasant experience than being alone in the desert.

Spend 40 days seeking The Lord. Spend 40 days loving The Lord with all your heart, strength, soul, and mind. After 40 days of seeking Him, you will have formed a habit which should be easier to continue. You will have your own evidence of the power of spending time seeking Him. My prayer is that, after 40 days, you will have found Jesus in a personal and powerful game changing way. And you will spend the rest of your life utilizing *The 40-Day Challenge* every day because it has become *"FUEL to Ignite Your Soul."*

THE CHALLENGE

Most everyone likes a challenge. Everyone knows a challenge can be fun, it can be serious, and it can take an unusual amount of determination and effort to complete. But the joy of completing a challenge makes it all worthwhile.

"The biggest impact The 40-Day Challenge had on me is in helping me to be more faithful and serious in my communication with God."

— Tim Urling, Missionary to Mexico

If you miss a day, keep going the next day. This is NOT the law, but rather a challenge. Like some medicines, it is best if you do not skip or miss a day; but if you do, just pick it up the next day until you complete the 40 days. If it takes you 50 days to complete *The 40-Day Challenge,* then so be it. Just keep going. Finishing is the most important part. *"Go to the end."*

I had more than one false start on my journey. It was hard to go from a dead stop spiritually to meeting daily with Jesus. When I switched from using a yellow pad to lined journals to write my prayers out word for word it made a big difference in my ability to write and keep my prayers in order and be able to re-read them. That was very helpful, but still, I struggled. Then I just let go and started telling God what I needed, like I would my best friend. For me, that made praying much easier and Scriptural.

"...Tell God what you need, and thank him for all he has done."
— Philippians 4:6

Also, the challenge is between you and the Lord, but sometimes we need encouragement and help to complete any challenge. We set up a system for that. Please stop and pick up your phone and text us right now. Text "40days" (no spacing) to 50700. We will text back some words of encouragement and touch base with you a few times to help you complete **The 40-Day Challenge**. So, stop reading, pick up your phone and text us right now!

"The goal of The 40-Day Challenge is
to bring you into a personal relationship with Jesus.
A powerful life altering, life-giving relationship
changing everything about you for eternity."
- Ross Alan Hill

Make your commitment, NOW. On the next page is a personal commitment for you to sign and date.

THE 40-DAY CHALLENGE FORMULA:
COMMITMENT

PERSONAL COMMITMENT

Yes, on this _____ *(Date),*

I _____ *(Name),*
commit to seek The Lord with all of my heart, all my strength, all my
soul, and all my mind.

Signature _____

Don't forget to pick up your phone and finish your commitment by texting "40days" (no spacing) to 50700.

CHAPTER 5

Pick A Time

PREPARATION TIME

John Wooden: Preparation is Everything

"Failing to prepare is preparing to fail."

— John Wooden
From his book, *Wooden: A Lifetime of Observations
and Reflections On and Off the Court*

The ten-time National Collegiate Athletic Association (NCAA) Coach, John Wooden, nicknamed the "Wizard of Westwood," is an icon for coaches of all sports. As a man of high moral standing and commitment, John Wooden's philosophy has reached outside the basketball court and into any practice.

Coach Wooden, believed first and foremost, in **preparation**; his entire coaching philosophy hinged on it. He was always more focused on what his team was going to do than what the other team would potentially do. He knew if his guys did their jobs to the best of their abilities, no one could beat them. For Wooden, this meant making sure his team was prepared.

This entailed doing everything right—from putting on socks to setting screens and how the team readied for each game.

Preparation is required in just about every facet of life and business. You must always be prepared. Being prepared spiritually— the most important area of your life—is of utmost importance.

— Clint Hurdle Daily Devotional - www.clinthurdle.com

PICK A TIME

As I reflected on my banking career, I noticed my calendar controlled my life for 40 years. I looked at my calendar every evening to help prepare me for the next day and seldom missed a meeting. I am pretty sure for most of us, your calendar is important in your life, too.

The 40-Day Challenge is about preparation! And preparation starts when you *pick a time of the day* to meet with The Lord. The time is up to you, but I recommend you *pick the same time every day.* For me, even though I am not a morning person, I picked 6:00 a.m. It is the best time for me to not have interruptions. I can be consistent with the time. It seldom conflicts with other demands on my schedule. What would be the best time for you?

For most people, it takes some effort to figure out what is the best time. Give it some thought, and then write it down in the space provided at the end of this chapter.

PUT IT ON YOUR CALENDAR

Next, put it on your calendar. Pick tomorrow as the day you start. How long are you going to spend with The Lord? I would recommend one hour, for now. I will explain the rest of the steps in the upcoming chapters, so you can adjust if you need to do so. But for now, plan for one hour.

Some of you may be thinking, one hour is a lot of time. I

suppose it is. But, if you are trying to fall in love with Jesus with all your heart, soul, strength, and mind, is one hour really much time? Just put the hour on your calendar for now. As I said, you can adjust if you need to as you move forward. It is of the utmost importance that you add the time to your calendar. Why? For most of us, our calendar controls our life. We keep up with all our appointments through our calendars. The calendar sends a reminder about appointments. Your calendar has been designed to help you be on time for your appointments and not to forget them by providing you with an alert.

Have you scheduled the meeting on your calendar?

Use your calendar to make sure you keep your appointment with Jesus. My calendar says "Preparation Time" on the title line and "My Deck/Office" for the location and it shows 6:00-8:00 a.m. for the time. I picked every day on the repeat section, so it is on my calendar seven days a week. I checked the unending box because I plan to never stop meeting with Jesus until I start meeting with Him in person in heaven.

By now, you'll be asking yourself if I realized I have repeated myself several times. The answer is *YES!* The reason I keep writing about putting it on your calendar is that I have learned that the people who don't put their meeting with Jesus on their calendar are the ones who fail to complete *The 40-Day Challenge* and, worse, they fail in building a personal relationship with Jesus. I don't want that to happen to you. So, please, put it on your calendar . . . NOW please!

As I was writing the last paragraph, my phone lit up reminding me of my 6:00 a.m. "Preparation Time" meeting with The Lord. It works! I must stop writing for now. I have an important meeting with Jesus.

WHAT IF YOU MISS A MEETING?

Have you ever missed an important meeting? What did it cost you? How did you recover? We have all done it. Many times, people give us grace but, sometimes, missing an important meeting ruins your chance for a nice new piece of business and/or a new relationship. One thing is for certain, you learn you never want to miss another important meeting! Being absolutely transparent, I have missed more than one important meeting over the years. And I have missed some with Jesus . . . but, He is full of grace.

I have also learned, my meeting with Jesus is the most important meeting I have every day. So, I need to schedule it on my calendar just like all the other meetings I have. I know that, if I do not, I will miss it. In my life, consistency is vital, what about your life? I also know the fact that if I do the most important thing in my day *first*, I will be much more productive the rest of the day.

When someone asks you to meet with them, you look at your calendar and you see all your appointments. You can see what time you have free on your calendar and you can offer those times for a meeting.

If you are serious about *completing The 40-Day Challenge*, you must schedule the time to meet with Jesus on your calendar seven days a week, so *you can build the rest of your life around your meetings with Him.*

THE 40-DAY CHALLENGE FORMULA:
COMMITMENT + QUALITY TIME

PICK A TIME TO MEET WITH JESUS

I will meet with Jesus from _____ to _____ every day.

I have placed this on my calendar seven days a week, every week.

Signature _____

CHAPTER 6

Pick A Place

MEETING PLACE

Every meeting on my calendar has a "meeting place." Some meetings are in my office, others are in the boardroom or in a conference room. Sometimes I meet with other executives in their offices. Sometimes, my clients come to my office to meet. Every meeting has a meeting place. In the same way, you need to pick a place for your meeting with Jesus.

It is not enough to pick a time; you must also know where you are meeting. It may involve driving time, so you would need to leave home early enough to be on time for your meeting with Jesus.

BE ON TIME

Do you show up late to meet with the chairman of your board or your largest customer? Of course not! Do you wonder where the meeting is going to be? No! You took care of the time and place details when you made the appointment. Do you show up late for a doctor's appointment? No! Are you late picking up the kids from school or practice? No! Do you show up late to preach? Of course not! I was a banker for 40 years and I never missed a board meeting, nor did I show up late. Not once!

It is the same with Jesus, you should have a consistent time and place to meet with Him. And please, do not cancel the meeting or show up late!

My favorite place to meet with Jesus is on my deck and I do it every morning, weather permitting. It is perfect, I can see the sunrise, hear the geese and ducks, sometimes I get to see deer. My deck is quiet with no interruptions. It is the perfect place for me to meet with Jesus. Pick a place and stick to it.

I once read an article about five keys to a successful lunch meeting. It piqued my interest because I met with clients over lunch most days. The article suggested a number of things to do. Arrive at the restaurant early. Make sure you get a table not a booth. Pick a table in a quiet place, like a corner. Put yourself in the corner seat so your guest is looking at you and will not be distracted by all of the activity of the restaurant. Arrange with your server for them to give you the check, not your guest. The writer said that your chances of success would greatly increase by following those rules. I immediately implemented the writer's five keys and started reaping the benefits. So, I also applied the same insights to my meetings with Jesus and they greatly impacted my spiritual life. In the same way, please take the time to think about where you are meeting with Jesus, just as you would an important customer.

Think through what would be a great time, location and set-up for your meeting with Jesus. It is your *most* important meeting of the day, so it demands careful planning to greatly enhance your chance of success.

A PLACE OF NO DISTRACTIONS

Ideally, you will employ the five keys of a successful lunch meeting to *The 40-Day Challenge*.

- Pick a place where you can be alone, with no distractions. No phones to disturb you.
- Turn your cell phone off or turn off notifications and turn your phone upside down.
- No computers sending out sound notifications or flashing screens.
- No employee or customer interruptions. No spouse or family interruptions.
- Just you, The Lord, your Bible, and your prayer journal.

Jesus loved to go to the mountains, the garden "a certain place" to be alone and pray. He often told his friends to wait while He went even further and prayed. He is showing us His love for nature, and he is showing us his desire to be alone in a place with no distractions. And, I might add, a beautiful place. Follow His examples.

Some guys like to tell me they pray in their car as they are driving. I have done that too. It might work in a pinch or for a short prayer before a meeting, but that is not the way to develop a deep relationship with Jesus. There are far too many distractions and way too many thoughts to be able to concentrate, much less hear His soft gentle voice.

Developing a quality relationship with Jesus requires some care, some thought, and some effort. It requires thinking about the ideal place to meet with Him. Jesus had a place to meet with God. You also need a place to meet with The Lord.

"After your talk on Luke 11, I read at least 12 different Bible translations. I was drawn to the opening, verse 1, and how Jesus 'prayed in a certain place,' when his disciples came to Him. Why use the adjective 'certain' unless it was a part of His morning routine? Every translation I read, but two, used the adjective. Since you have always led us to read The Word and to pray in a regular or certain place – at a certain time, I just want to tell you thank you for your witness."
— Ron Harris, Partner of CFO-Partner
Survivor of Delta Air Lines Flight 191 Crash
Dallas/Fort Worth International Airport August 2, 1985

You need a physical location to meet with God every day, at an appointed time, where you read and study His Word. Both are essential to your relationship with Jesus. This is the place where you come into His presence for prayer. My experiences tell me the highest place where the two intersect is where you build your relationship with The Lord. Did you see the movie *Prayer Warrior*? If not, go rent and watch this wonderfully portrayed.

I have found my physical location where I meet with The Lord every day becomes holy ground and can be sensed by those who are sensitive to the Holy Spirit. It is the place where I read the Word of God and pray to The Lord. I am always surprised when this happens, but should I be? Just picture this in your mind…you are in your private place with the Bible open and prayers on your lips. You, my friend, are in your own personal Throne Room of God Almighty—a Holy Place. There can be no higher place for you and me than to be alone with The Lord of All, reading His Word and conversing with our Maker. There God speaks wisdom and understanding through His Word and through our prayers.

It becomes our own Holy place to meet with God. I believe some people can sense His presence because of all the time spent with The Lord, reading the Word and praying in my certain, special place. It is not about me, it is about Him.

Where else could be a *"higher point along the way?"* Where else could wisdom and understanding intersect in such a powerful way?

I am not a Bible scholar, but I am convinced wisdom and understanding come to us at that certain place and the exact time where we, as individuals, commune with our Lord. I believe there are numerous Scriptures in the Bible that support my hypothesis.

"Blessing live in the land of obedience."
— Ross Alan Hill

For years, my wife and I were the first ones to arrive at the bank in the morning. I met with The Lord in my office from 7:00-9:00 a.m. daily. Do not let the two hours scare you. I met with a group of Christian executives in Dallas last year. When they saw my calendar and understood I had two hours set aside to meet with Jesus every day, they interrupted my presentation to discuss, in detail, how I could do such a thing. I told them I did not start out doing two hours, but that it had developed over time. They were in disbelief. They just could not understand how a busy, successful, and growing company with a nationwide footprint could have its CEO spend two hours a day with The Lord. I explained to them my company's success was explicitly linked to my spiritual life. My next book is all about how to use your life and business for the Lord. It is due out in late 2022. To get more info and to pre-order **God's Economy**, go to www. RossAlanHill.com/economy.

> "I have so much to do today that
> I'm going to need to spend three hours in prayer
> in order to be able to get it all done."
> — Martin Luther

Allow me to reassure you, when I first started meeting with The Lord, I was doing well if the meeting lasted fifteen minutes. But over time, the meetings began lasting longer and longer. If I got done early, it was okay. It only meant I had a little extra time in my day.

Just yesterday, one of my clients, a successful CEO, told me about spending over two hours with The Lord the morning before our meeting. When he realized how long he had met with The Lord he could hardly believe it. He said the time flew by.

Where is your certain place?

THE 40-DAY CHALLENGE FORMULA:
COMMITMENT + TIME + PLACE

I commit to meet with Jesus every day at _____.

Signature _____

CHAPTER 7

A Chapter A Day

"Ross, when I first met with one of our new clients, she readily admitted she hadn't been reading her Bible and didn't feel a connection to God as she once did.

I encouraged her with The 40-Day Challenge and when she came tonight for coaching, she could hardly get the words out fast enough to tell me all God was teaching her. There were pages and pages written in her journal of all she was learning."

— A Tall Oaks Coach

_____

ONE-YEAR BIBLE READING PLANS

Personally, I do not like one-year Bible reading plans one bit! Why? Because reading the Bible **should not be a race**. It should be *quality* time, not *quantity* time. I recommend a slow reflective time, where you seek The Lord. Seek to understand. Seek the Holy Spirit to teach you from His Word. A time where you can think about what you are reading and think about the things God is putting into your mind as you read. A time to enjoy the richness of the Word of God. I have many driven men and women, some of America's top professionals in their fields, as clients. Most run hard and fast. I often coach these elite performers using the concept, *Slow Down to Speed Up*. When this concept is applied, it is a game-changer for most. It is very difficult for hard charging executives to slow down. It does not come naturally for them. I promise my clients, this strategty dramatically improves both personal and company performance. And as you know, I personally guaranteed the same results (page xi) for you in this area of your Spiritual life.

It was really hard for me to settle in and trust this concept. I could feel my mind wanting to speed on. It was as though I was a race car at the starting line revving up my engine with my right foot on the gas while my left foot was planted securely on the break waiting for the green light to flash.

"As a race car driver, driving is the easy part.
The hard part is containing the emotions on the track."
— Kevin Harvick, NASCAR Champion
720 Races, 58 Wins, 391 Top Ten Finishes, 31 Poles
Nicknamed "The Closer and "Happy Harvick"

IT NEVER GETS OLD

There are 1,189 chapters in the Bible. If you read one chapter a day, it will take you 3.2 years to read the Bible cover to cover one time. I have been reading one or two chapters a day for over a decade. My wife and I have a goal to read an individual Bible for each of our 17 grandchildren and each of our children before we die. It is our way of sharing our faith with them. I pray The Lord gives me the time to do so.

Reading God's Word over and over never gets old. It never feels like I have read it before. Instead, it comes alive with fresh new insights and new information every time I read it. Just a few days ago, I read Matthew chapter 15 and jotted down four thoughts from the chapter I had never had before. This morning I read The Book of Mark chapter 8 and noticed 16 questions in one chapter. I never recognized the significance nor the number before. Each of those questions are important and we should be answering each of them ourselves.

How is it possible, you ask? The Word of God is living and breathing, and our life is, as well, so circumstances change. The Word reveals things we need to know on a continual basis. The Word is alive, and it speaks to the soul in marvelous new ways each time we read it. The Word of God is truth and thus an absolute authority. The Bible is the *gold standard* for truth.

"Heaven and earth will disappear,
but my words will never disappear."

— Matthew 24:35

One of my mentors, a man I love very much wrote the following to me:

"The Bible gives me life, and direction and
promises for the day, and opens opportunities every single day
to make use of them. I take one full hour (or more)
every single day to read the Bible
because it is a delight for me and
speaks to my heart and mind."

—Dr. Enrique Cepeda, Director
The Thomas School of International Studies,
Mid-America Christian University

I found once I stopped reading the Bible fast and slowed down, I discovered amazing things. Small hidden gems of truth. Many times, these were simple, yet profound insights.

NEW THINGS I DISCOVERED

Here is a partial list of what I discovered the last time I read the first couple of chapters of the Book of Genesis:

- God used the word "light" nine times and "lights" three more times in the first chapter.
- The first words God spoke, "Let there be light, and there was light. God saw that the light was good." (Genesis 1:3) This was the first time He said something was good.
- He said six times His creation was good, but when He looked at what He created in the whole, He said it was VERY GOOD.
- The first time He said something was not good was when He said it was not good for man to be alone.
- So, God fixed it through the first surgery ever (Genesis 2:18-24).
- He created a woman from the rib of a man.
- He put trees in the garden. Some think there were only two. I do not. I believe there were many more. Only God knows for sure. Do you know how many species of trees there are? More than you can shake a stick at! 60,065 different kinds of trees! I do not know about you, but this sure changes my view of the size of the Garden of Eden!
- The very first question ever asked by God is in chapter 3.
- I discovered there are one hundred and sixty one "first" in the first 4 chapters of Genesis.
- Number one hundred and six is the first time people prayed to The Lord.
- The first time He referred to himself in the plural since using the word "Us" as the Father, Son and Holy Spirit.

HOW MANY OF THESE?

Now ask yourself this question: how many of these things have you ever thought about? How many of these things did you know? Trust me, I never saw these details before, not until I slowed down to not just read but to *notice* what God was saying. When I noticed, I realized how awesome our God is and what He created for us is amazing!

I believe if you are *speed* reading through the verses of the Bible, you are going to miss many of the gems God has placed there for us.

ONE DAY – ONE CHAPTER

The 40-Day Challenge is all about reading just one chapter, and absolutely no more than two chapters a day. Start each reading with a short prayer. Ask God to show you something you did not know, or to reveal a new treasure from His Word to you, or a new application from His Word to your life. One of my clients has a program in his church called "Turn the Page." That is about what a chapter a day amounts to. Just turn the page every day. How easy is that?

When I read the Bible, I have a pen and a highlighter nearby. I write all kinds of notes. I highlight and underline the parts of the Scriptures that speak to me. The things God is teaching me about Him or how to live for Him, or about how to live life. (Please go to this link to see helpful photos www.rossalanhill. com/bible) Many think my Bible looks like a college textbook!

God inspired the authors to write the Bible—all 40 of them over a time span of 1,500 years. The entire Bible is the inspired, inerrant Word of God, written for the purpose of us to know our Creator. I want to read it and feel it like a warm ocean wave as it rolls over me. I want it to go deep into my mind, my heart, and my soul. To know Him and to have wisdom and understanding about how to live for Him, obey Him, serve Him, and worship Him.

"The Bible is such an invigorating and tremendous staple in my life. It gives hope when I feel all is lost and breath when circumstances hold my head underwater. However, the Word of God brings healing to my soul in times I need restoration from the tumultuous fight life brings. The Word of God my — mmmmmmmm Good!"
— Quinton Decker
Pastor, Hickman Road Church of Christ

Start your reading with the Book of Genesis or Matthew. You decide. Please keep reading one chapter after another, one day at a time. Do not skip around. Just start reading and keep going; so by the end of the 40 days, you will have read 40 consecutive chapters. Let the Word get deep into your heart and soul by taking time to read, comprehend and let the Holy Spirit lead you to a deeper understanding.

MAKE NOTES

Go to your local Christian bookstore or online to buy some *Bible pens* and *Bible-Hi-Gliders* to write notes in your Bible and to highlight verses that have special meaning to you (see chapter 13).

As an example, I write all kinds of notes in the white margins of my Bible – notes like I listed earlier from the first chapter of Genesis. I also highlight verses or words that God points out to me, like the word "light." I have every word form of the word *light* highlighted in orange in my Bible. "Why orange?" you ask. No reason other than the color stuck out to me and I decided to use orange to make the words more noticeable. (Please go to this link to see helpful photos www.rossalanhill.com/bible)

I have every question in the Bible highlighted in blue. It is amazing how many questions there are in the Bible! In Genesis alone, there are 136 questions! (I have not audited the number, so I might be off just a bit.) There are twenty six questions in the first four chapters of Romans alone. I plan to write a book about the great questions from the Bible too.

Why do I highlight the questions? Because I noticed them when I slowed down. God wanted me to see them. One thing I have noticed is many of them are applicable in the middle of this COVID-19 pandemic and the current civil and global unrest. Have you ever noticed the questions? I never did until I was nearing the end of a Bible I was reading for my granddaughter Kara. So, this time as I am reading through a Bible for my granddaughter Presley, I have highlighted and counted every question. God brought them to my attention. The Lord wanted me to notice the many questions. I believe He is teaching me through these questions.

SLOW DOWN = SPEEDING UP

Are you getting the idea? Do you see where I am going? When we race through God's Word, we miss so much. We need to approach our faith like we approach the people we love.

I love my wife. I, therefore, know she will always answer my question with a question. She never wants to say where she wants to go out to eat; she wants me to make the decision. I know my wife loves Milky Way candy bars, and she loves a triple venti breve no foam latte with one Sweet'N Low. I know she will reheat the drink dozens of times in a day. She makes one venti last *all* day. She loves the color black and her clothes prove it, but she will deny it. And she loves to hear me laugh. She loves to serve people, she loves to take the high road, and she always sees the glass half-full. She always makes the bed when she gets up, and she hates being short—all 4'11 ½" of her. R.J. loves sauces and salad dressings and she always orders extra.

She finds great joy in her grandkids and in feeding ducks and the two geese she named Bill and Janet after our neighbors. Bill is not particularly fond of geese and I am not either, for that matter. She thought our neighbors would enjoy being teased, and she was right. She loves The Lord and is faithful to read His Word and prays daily. She is as beautiful on the inside as she is on the outside.

We have been commanded to love the Lord first and foremost. What does The Lord love? Do you know? Can you make a list? Try right now in the space provided below. What do *you* know The Lord loves?

_____

_____

_____

_____

_____

_____

_____

_____

_____

_____

THE 40-DAY CHALLENGE FORMULA:
COMMITMENT + TIME + PLACE +
READ ONE CHAPTER EACH DAY

Which book are you going to start with, The Book of Genesis or Matthew?

I commit to read only one chapter each day, starting with chapter 1 of the Book of _____ . I will continue reading one additional chapter each day for 40 days.

Signature _____

CHAPTER 8

Pray Using a Prayer Journal

PRAYER JOURNALS

Mark Batterson, author and pastor of the National Community Church in Washington, DC, taught me the importance of using a prayer journal. I have met with Mark dozens of times and he *always* has his prayer journal with him. This bestselling author and pastor wrote my all-time favorite book, which happens to be about prayer. *The Circle Maker* is a *New York Times* bestseller. This book expanded my concept of prayer by challenging me to *"pray bold prayers."* It helped me to understand *"my prayers never die."* It taught me that the prayers I have prayed for our kids and grandkids will outlive me as God will continue to answer my prayers long after I die. *"It is never too late to start praying about something."* The list of things he taught me goes on and on. Mark's book energized my prayer life. If you have not read *The Circle Maker*, please do. I believe it will have a special, positive impact on your life.

As you read earlier, I write my prayers out word for word.

I capture every thought, every word. I don't worry too much about spelling or run-on sentences. I just make sure to capture every word of my prayers.

I buy lined journals at the local bookstore or office supply store. They work great. I have tried all kinds of journals and sizes, but I won't attempt to tell you which is best for you. It is a personal choice. (Please go to this link to see helpful photos: www.rossalanhill.com/journals)

My prayer journals are my most precious possession save my Bible. As a precaution, I put my name and phone number in the front of every journal, just in case I lose it. I never have lost a journal, but I want to increase the possibility of getting it back if I ever do misplace one. I never pack my journals in a suitcase; instead, I put them in my carry-on bag. I date the first right-hand page. I start my writing by notating the Scripture reference I read that day. As an example, today I read John 21. Then I write a particular verse that meant a great deal to me that day.

"Then the disciple Jesus loved,"

— John 21:7

Then I write a little bit about why or how God spoke to me through this Scripture. As an example, I wrote the following in my prayer journal:

> *The phrase, then the disciple Jesus loved, appears five times in the Book of John but, interestingly, it never gives credit to John as the one who said it. Most scholars think it was John who wrote it and I think they are correct. But, as I ponder on the statement, I personalized it: Ross . . . the disciple Jesus loved.*

As I typed those words, I had chills and the hair on the back of my neck stood up. I got emotional . . . to think He loves me like that, despite all my sin and weakness. It is hard for me to comprehend, impossible to fully comprehend.

I think we should all personalize his statement by adding our own name:

_____ , *the disciple Jesus loved.*

When we do, we cannot avoid seeing how rich Jesus' love is for us.

YOU are the disciple He loved.

When you personalize the phrase, you begin to fully comprehend His love and devotion for you on a personal level. I believe it will bless your soul like nothing ever has before.

I would challenge you to ponder the idea that YOU are the one He loves. It changes everything when we see *ourselves through such a lens of truth.*

Most of the statements about the disciple Jesus loved occurred at the end of His life on *earth.* The battle to complete His mission was real. The pain He endured was both physical and emotional and it took all that was within Him to finish His race. He did it out of obedience and love for us.

The next step is to start praying, writing your prayers out word for word. *Perhaps you would like to take a moment right now to stop reading and pray to thank Jesus for loving you. Praise Him for that gift and reassurance.*

I TOOK MARK'S ADVICE

Mark Batterson personally challenged me to take notes like a world class journalist. He encouraged me to record, in my prayer journal, how God answers my prayers in full detail. When, where, and how, including all the many details. Mark said if I did, I would see just how mighty God is and how much He loves me. I took his advice.

A few years ago, several people remarked 2009 seemed

to have been a significant year in my life. I had no idea what they were talking about. Micah McGahan, one of the "Nation Changers" I mentor, commented about it several times. One day he asked, "What happened in 2009 that changed you?" I could not tell him. So, I decided I to go back and re-read my 2009 prayer journal. I wondered if God was trying to show me something. To my surprise, I recorded two and half pages of prayers God had answered from my 2009 prayer journal specific to ME. Since people were telling me something had changed me, I only read the sections of my prayer journal about me. Prayers that I had prayed about me. I typed bullet points on each one of the prayers God had answered. I had no memory of praying most of the prayers.

"...Father, thank you for hearing me, You always hear me,"

— John 11:41 & 42

We suffer from information overload today. The typical Sunday *New York Times* newspaper contains more information than an adult could read in their entire lifetime back in the 1700's. Because we suffer from information overload, there is no possible way for someone to remember all their specific prayers. But, when you record your prayers using a prayer journal, keep the journals, and go back and read them, you will discover they are full of *FUEL to Ignite Your Soul.*

Your prayer journals provide a personal, and highly valuable, resource: a personal testimony about your relationship with God. A prayer journal allows you to see that God is alive, He hears your prayers, and He answers your prayers. You can record on the left-hand page, opposite your prayer, the details of how God answered your prayers. It is your *personal* proof positive and NO ONE can refute the evidence. Not even Satan.

SOME EXAMPLES

Here are some examples from my prayer journal of prayers I forgot I had prayed:

In March of 2009, I prayed about getting a *"Spiritual Whatsit"* for my office. A Spiritual Whatsit is something you put into your office, home, or car; and when someone sees it, they ask, *"What-is-it?"* Then you explain what it is and how you use it for sharing your faith. Six months later, in September of 2009, I commissioned a Redento Raffinato, a hand-blown, 33 inch vase, blown from broken pieces of glass to be my *"Spiritual Whatsit."* I put it in my office on October 7, 2009. Since then, I have shared the story of redemption with over 3,000 first-time visitors to my office. I did not remember praying about it in March of 2009 until I re-read my prayer journal. (Please go to this link to see helpful photos www.rossalanhill.com/redento)

On July 31, 2009, I prayed about writing a book. I was 56 years old, and I did not even know how to spell my middle name correctly; but there I was, praying about writing a book! As I re-read my 2009 prayer journal, I had two thoughts. First, I had no memory of praying about writing a book. The second was that the date when I prayed about writing a book was close to the date I started writing my first book, *Broken Pieces – Nothing is Wasted.* So, I checked my manuscript and discovered I wrote the first chapter of my first book in the first week of August 2013, four years and one week after my prayer in 2009! Can you believe it? Only God can do these things. Talk about fuel! My heart raced when I realized what God had done. My prayer journals documented what would have been impossible to pinpoint and know.

On September 14, 2009, I prayed about raising $300,000 to drill water wells in third world countries. I did not own a passport. I had never been out of the country. Why would I be praying about such a thing? On November 30, 2009, I went on a mission trip to the Dominican Republic. As a result, $68,000 was raised to help a church install a water treatment plant to provide safe, clean water for their community. Since then, my wife and I have given or helped raise $450,000 for water wells. Today, about 150,000 people drink clean, safe, fresh water as a result of a prayer in September of 2009!

"Your prayer life and the trajectory of your spiritual life are explicitly tied together."

— Ross Alan Hill

IGNITE YOUR SOUL

One of my clients sent this unsolicited text to me today..."*I have been utilizing my prayer journal more and it has been a huge blessing! Reading entries I made from a year ago and [I am] almost in tears seeing how much God has moved and answered prayers in my life! I'm reminded of His faithfulness and reinvigorated by it!*"

Mark was right! A prayer journal, done well, will *ignite your soul!* It allows you to see that God is alive. He hears your prayers, and He answers your prayers. Without my prayer journal, I would not have known these things, simply because I did not remember these prayers. It would have been lost to me and to the world. *Slow Down to Speed Up!* But, with a prayer journal, I have *proof* of God being actively involved in my life! That is *FUEL To Ignite Your Soul.*

"I have found it a great blessing to treasure up in the memory, the answers God graciously gives me in answer to prayer. I have always kept a record to strengthen the memory. I advise the keeping of a little memorandum book. On one side — say the left-handside — put down the petition, and the date when you began to offer it. Let the opposite page be left blank to put down the answer in each case, and you will soon find how many answers you get, and thus you will be encouraged more and more, you faith will be strengthened; and especially you will see what a lovely, bountiful and gracious Being God is; your heart will go out more and more in love to God, and you will say – it is my Heavenly Father Who has been so kind, I will trust in Him, I will confide in him through His Son."

— George Muller (www.georgemuller.org)

THE 40-DAY CHALLENGE FORMULA:

COMMITMENT + TIME + PLACE + ONE CHAPTER EACH DAY + PRAY USING A PRAYER JOURNAL

I commit to writing out my prayers word for word every day of The 40-Day Challenge.

Signature _____

Date _____

CHAPTER 9

Top 12 Surprises of Using a Prayer Journal

I LOVE BEING SURPRISED

As you will remember from Chapter One, I started writing my prayers out word for word to help me concentrate and build a prayer life. The prayer journal was a tool to help me stay on track and keep my mind from drifting. It was not until Mark Batterson wrote *The Circle Maker,* and coached me up, that I became a faithful user/proponent of the prayer journal. Little did I realize the many surprises that would flow out of the use of a prayer journal. Following is a list of my Top 12 Surprises:

- **Surprise 1.** Other than my Bible, my prayer journals are my most precious possession.
- **Surprise 2.** Just seeing them gives me a huge amount of comfort.
- **Surprise 3.** They are my personal evidence that God is alive. No one, no government nor any power can dispute my evidence.
- **Surprise 4.** My prayer journals have taught me that my prayers never die. Every time I re-read any of my prayer

journals, I see more of my prayers answered, and some were answered repeatedly.

- **Surprise 5.** My prayer journals helped me to see my prayer life was very self-centered, which helped me to broaden my prayers to pray for others.
- **Surprise 6.** When I re-read my prayer journals, many times I have no memory of praying about the things I am reading or what motivated me to pray about them. Yet, many times God has used those prayers to make huge differences in my life and others. How did that happen? It is amazing that He never forgets our prayers, but we do!
- **Surprise 7.** The things on which I placed great emphasis or urgency on in my prayers, God has not yet answered or answered in ways that were directly opposite my request. More importantly, if He answered it the way I had asked, it would have been a disaster.
- **Surprise 8.** The things I feared most were often things which had no permanent or lasting negative effect on my life or on others.
- **Surprise 9.** When some people walk by my prayer journals, they stop in their tracks because they instantly feel the presence of The Lord. This has happened on more than one occasion. Wow!
- **Surprise 10.** For me, my prayer journal is the *FUEL to Ignite My Soul.* No other human item has done more to energize my faith. When combined with reading my Bible, my journals have become my personal "burning bush."
- **Surprise 11.** I never thought I would ever teach, let alone write a book, about a method that thousands utilize daily to have an amazing relationship with Jesus.
- **Surprise 12.** Some friends are building special cabinets

in their homes to store their prayer journals for safety and to pass their faith on to their children and grandchildren.

IT IS NOT THAT HARD

I bought a lined journal at a bookstore and started writing my prayers out word for word, like a letter. I only write my prayers on the right-hand page. It was difficult for me to write on the left page because the journal did not lay flat. I use the left-hand page for other things I will tell you about it later. For now, put the date on the top of the right-hand page. I use a red pen to write out all my prayers. You can use whatever color you like, but only use one color to write your prayers. (www.RossAlanHill.com/journals)

Use the second colored pen, black in my case, to write only on the left- hand page how God answered your prayers on the right-hand page. Be very specific and detailed.

Sometimes I will hear The Lord speak to me in a whisper. He might bring to my mind a Scripture, a story, a date, or a name. I write it in black on the left-hand page, too. The left-hand page has lots of excellent uses and while it may seem like you are wasting paper, over the years you will see how little waste there is, and you will find the left page to be invaluable. The left-hand page makes it crystal clear when I go back to read my prayer journal what I prayed and how God responded. (www. RossAlanHill.com/journalsset2)

IT IS SO SIMPLE, EVEN A SEVEN YEAR OLD CAN DO IT

One of my CEO clients, Denver Green, started *The 40-Day Challenge* and it has dramatically changed his life. He taught it to his wife and she, too, started changing as a result. She passed it to her 11-year-old son and he experienced Jesus as never before, accepting him as Lord and Savior. He continues to use *The 40-Day Challenge* every day.

Soon, their 7-year-old son Eli asked his dad for a prayer

journal. He wanted to participate in *The 40-Day Challenge*, too. His dad thought it was cool but let the idea die thinking Eli was a little too young. However, Eli was determined to get a prayer journal. He was at his friend's house and his friend's dad Jason (Denver's business partner) took them to Wal-Mart to buy a toy. Eli asked Jason if he could buy a prayer journal instead of a toy. When Eli came home with a prayer journal, he could hardly wait to show it to his dad. His dad was pleasantly surprised and humbled. He said to Eli, "Let's go buy a new Bible to go along with your prayer journal and when we get back, I will teach you how to do *The 40-Day Challenge.*"

They went to Mardel Christian Book Store, and bought Eli a new Bible. His dad taught him how to read his children's Bible and how to use the prayer journal. Instead of reading one chapter a day, Eli started reading one verse a day. He uses the right-hand page just like his family to record his prayers. He saves the left-hand page for God's answers to his prayers.

Below is a photo of Eli reading his Bible to me and another one of him showing me his prayer journal. (Please go to this link to see helpful photos www.rossalanhill.com/eli)

On October 15, 2020, I was coaching Denver when he told me Eli was very happy at breakfast. His dad asked him why he was grinning from ear to ear and Eli said, "I finished reading the New Testament this morning!" Denver was thrilled and told his son to come and sit in his dad's chair for breakfast to celebrate his accomplishment! How cool is that?

I wrote Eli a note and previewed what he was going to read Friday morning. Eli is now 9 years old. He started reading one verse a day when he was 7. He has been falling in love with Jesus one verse a day! A perfect example of how to Slow Down to Speed Up or to use Mark Batterson's title to his newest book, Eli is forming a habit to *Win The Day*.

It's an even better example of a mom and dad "training up a child in the way he should go!" According to Barna Group and the American Bible Society, only 9 percent of U.S. adults read the Bible daily. Are you in their number?

CHAPTER 10

His Presence

When you read the Bible about people falling to the ground in the presence of The Lord, what comes to your mind? Do you wonder if you will ever feel the need to fall on the ground in His presence? Do you wonder what caused the men and women written about in the Bible to do it? Do you ever wonder why they do it? Do you wonder what it is about being in The Lord's presence that caused them to respond in such a way? I sure do.

Have you ever wondered what it must be like to be in His presence? Will you fall to the ground? Will you be overwhelmed? What will you feel?

I have hoped for a personal friendship, a close one, a best friend type of relationship. The type where I could even tease him a bit because He likes the way I use sarcasm. I have wondered all kinds of things. If I told you all my questions, you might have confirmation of my need for a therapist!

The physical presence of God is not available to us right now, but His Spiritual presence is totally available. In fact, He promised it.

> *"If you look for me wholeheartedly, you will find me.*
> *I will be found by you, says the Lord."*
> — Jeremiah 29:13-14

I can think of no better way to find The Lord than to seek Him every day by reading the Bible and praying using a prayer journal. Looking for Jesus wholeheartedly cannot be done in an inadequate, incomplete, helter-skelter basis.

> *"I love all who love me. Those who search will surely find me."*
> — Proverbs 8:17

There are more Scriptures to support this truth. We cannot search and find Jesus if we neglect to spend time with Him or overlook Him.

> *"A Love for Jesus is not found in the land of neglect."*
> — Ross Alan Hill

I also believe we enter the throne room when we open the Word of God and read it to understand and seek Him. We continue to seek Him as we pray and as we listen intently for His small, sweet whispers. When we regularly approach The Lord using these methods, we will find Him. He promises it. God never promises anything He does not do. He delivers on His promises 100% of the time.

I have been practicing *The 40-Day Challenge* for more than a decade and I am in His presence nearly every day. The same is true for my wife. I have taught this method over and over. It is simple. It is basic. And hundreds of people report being in His presence as a result.

Scores of people have come into my former office and told me:

"There is something special about your office."

"I feel the presence of The Lord in your office."

"I feel the presence of the Holy Spirit in your office."

"I feel the peace of God in your office."

"Do you pray a lot in your office?"

"Could you pray for me?"

These individuals are much more sensitive to the presence of The Lord than me. They are drawn to my office and sense they are on holy ground. It has nothing to do with me and everything to do with hours of reading the Scriptures and praying in that office. Most did not know it was the place where I met with Jesus every day. They just sensed it was a Holy place. They were taken aback by feeling His presence so strongly in a bank, much less the President and CEO's office.

I have no explanation for it, except that it was used, not only for my personal time with The Lord, but all day long to pray for employees, customers, friends, and issues we were facing in running our business.

How does it happen? I do not know. Can it happen in your office? I do not know. Will it happen on my deck and in my new office? I do not know. I certainly hope all these things happen. Why? Because it brings joy to the people who experience it and it brings joy to me to know the Holy Spirit's presence is being felt so mightily.

I cannot reproduce such a thing. There is no known formula to recreate it. It is not because my spiritual life is so great. I sin just like everyone else. In fact, sometimes I feel like I must be the worst sinner of all time.

I just know this: It is very humbling when people say those things to me. I give 100% of the praise to The Lord. I am committed to loving The Lord with all my heart, soul, mind, and strength and to loving others as I love myself. I am committed to seeking Him first. To do it all, I utilize *The 40-Day Challenge.*

CHAPTER 11

Hope and Encouragement

DEVOTIONS

A dear friend of mine and I were playing golf in California recently when Chris asked how my new book was going. He wanted to know how long the "devotion" would take each day.

In one way, Chris' question was off track, and in another, marvelous way, he was spot on!

Normally, when I think of a devotion, I think of it as something like a thought for the day. A Scripture or two and a short thought to frame the day, along with a prayer. But the word "devotion" has another meaning, too. It means *a profound dedication or consecration to a person* and, in this case, the person is Jesus. And that is exactly what *The 40-Day Challenge* is all about.

If we are going to have an earnest and profound dedication to The Lord, it is not going to be limited in time or scope!

Meaningful relationships are not built overnight nor are they built on limited exposure. Genuinely great relationships are built on quantity *and* quality of time. They are built on both good and rough days. They are built in sickness and in health.

They are built amid trials and triumphs. In fact, I believe most of my growth in my relationship with Jesus has come on my most difficult days. It has come in the midst of heartaches, crushing attacks, and failures. That is when I have needed Him most. When the good times roll, we can think we are invincible. We can believe we do not need to walk with Him so closely. We can become full of pride and think, "I've got this, I don't need The Lord." I have first-hand experience in both and have found all of this to be true in my search for a deeper relationship with God.

I do not want to come across as having it all together. When I say I am still learning and growing, I am! I have a great deal of both to do. Nor do I want the methods taught here to be considered the "only way" or the "law." No, this is just *my way*. My way has worked for over 1,000 people. It worked for me, my wife, my friends, business leaders, and spiritual leaders, all of whom I coach. It has worked in India and China and Africa and in Europe. It works here in Oklahoma, too. The people it worked for wanted me to write about it so they could pass it on to their families, friends, neighbors, and co-workers.

I attended a luncheon recently to hear Curtis Bowers speak. He is smart and his talk was amazing. This man has done so much research. His presentation was eye-opening and informative. In his talk, he stated he believes over 50% of the pastors and 90% of the folks in church do not have a personal relationship with Jesus. My experience tells me he is almost right. I would say it might be closer to 90% in both categories. Remember, *I once lived that way*. I can spot it in others. It is not a slam nor a criticism but rather an observation. Being a pastor may be one of the most difficult careers/callings in the world. The demands and the pressure are huge. Sometimes, the personal relationship with Jesus just gets pushed out of their lives. Like every one of us, pastors are very busy. Most work six plus days a week. But there is hope for all of us. It does not have to be that way. You can know Jesus up close and personal. Just implement and practice *The 40-Day Challenge because it is "FUEL to Ignite Your Soul."*

It starts with setting a daily meeting with Jesus that cannot be canceled for any reason.

A. Pick a **time**

B. Pick a **place**

C. **Calendar** your meeting seven days a week for eternity

D. Be on time and **keep** your appointment

E. Read only **one to two chapters** a day from the Bible

F. **Write** out your prayers word for word in a **prayer journal**

G. **Listen** for his gentle whispers

Jesus loves you. He wants you to love Him. Living in *relationhip* with Jesus is just that simple.

"For God so loved the world, that he gave his only Son,
that whoever believes in him shall not perish but have eternal life."
— John 3:16 (NIV)

Jesus was asked which is the greatest commandment. Jesus said it was to *"Love the Lord your God with all your heart and with all of your soul and with all of your mind and with all of your strength."* He went on to say, the second is this, *"You shall love your neighbor as you love yourself."*

He also said, *"Seek first the kingdom of God and his righteousness, and all these things will be added to you."*

Blessings live in the land of obedience.

At one point, the Bible tells us even His disciples asked, *"Who is this man?"* Are you asking the same question today? Jesus Christ is the Son of God, and He came to save *you* so you can live eternally in heaven with Him as your Lord and Savior. All you have to do is admit you are a sinner, repent (turn away) from your sins, ask the Lord Jesus to forgive you, and ask Him to come into your heart and be your Lord and Savior.

Tell a friend who is a believer, ask them to disciple you in the ways of the Lord, and ask them to take you to church. Publicly accept The Lord and be baptized.

Then start spending time with Jesus every day by practicing *The 40-Day Challenge.*

Today, I recognize I am a sinner. I repent of my sins and I have asked Jesus into my life as my Lord and Savior.

Signature _____

Date _____

CHAPTER 12

David's Prayer Journal

DAVID'S EXAMPLES

The mechanics of a prayer journal are not difficult. I believe much of Psalms is David's prayer journal. Thus, the Book of Psalms is an excellent example of how to keep a prayer journal. David used almost every aspect of prayer in the Book of Psalms. In fact, if I counted correctly, there are 33 prayers in the Book of Psalms alone. I believe there are 650 prayers in the Bible and there are 25 different times Jesus prayed in the New Testament. Prayer is obviously a central theme of our Spiritual lives.

Have you ever asked yourself this question? "How did David become a man after God's own heart?" I have. It is an interesting question to reflect on and it is far deeper than David's lineage. Some of my thoughts are the size of his faith in God. He believed with God's help he could do anything. His faith led him to volunteer to fight Goliath while everyone else was too scared. He also demonstrated his desire to do the next right thing as documented in the Scriptures. But David was also a sinner and the Bible is certainly forthcoming on those issues.

I believe God viewed King David in the whole and not by one event. God knew him as a lowly shepherd boy, alone with the sheep under the starlit skies, perhaps where David learned to hear God's whispers. Maybe this is where he started to write his amazing prayers out word for word in his journal. Potentially all of these nights led to a heart connection with The

Lord Almighty which very likely caused God to say, "I have found David, the son of Jesse, a man after my own heart. He *will do everything I want him to do.*" - Acts 13:22 The Bible says, he who is without sin cast the first stone. We have all sinned and fallen short of the Glory of God. The Bible also says he knows our hearts and he forgives those who repent. David publically declared his faith as he worshipped The Lord.

David's prayer life almost perfectly illustrates how to pray. He praises God, thanks God, confesses his sins, asks God to forgive him, and shares his doubts. He complains to God and asks questions of God. David also asks God for help and miracles. He asks God to defend him, to show up and fight his battles, and he asks for wisdom and strength. The Book of Psalms is David's prayer journal to a large extent and is a great model for us. David simply wrote down his conversations with The Lord. He showed us a great method of writing them down. We can learn a lot from David, including how to pray and how to write your prayers out by reading the Book of Psalms.

David teaches us that God still speaks. David encourages and trains us how to have a relationship with The Lord. In Psalm 3, do you notice how he is, basically, just writing his prayers down like he is having a conversation with The Lord in his living room? Like he is writing a letter back home? You can see the conversation continue as he asks The Lord four questions in Psalm 4. In Psalm 5, David asks the Lord Almighty to *"Pay attention to my groaning."* He goes on to ask, *"Listen to my voice in the morning, Lord."* These are just a few examples of David's prayers.

Think about these questions:

- How do David's prayers compare to your prayers?
- Is that how you pray?
- What can you learn from his examples?
- Should you incorporate these examples into your prayer life?

If you will write your prayers out word for word like David did, you will be able to read and reflect on them. I believe you will have insights about where you are weak and what you need to work on in your prayer life. You might just learn where you are strong, too.

You will see for yourself, if you do what Paul instructed us to do when we pray. Paul said the following:

"Don't worry about anything,
instead, pray about everything.
Tell God what you need
and thank him for all he has done."

— Philippians 4:6

Does this seem like your prayer life? I know for years the few prayers I did pray were very weak. They were silly prayers and made no real difference in my life, or in the lives of others, and certainly were not worthy of eternity. I am sure my prayers were so ineffective, watered down, and useless they made God sleepy. No wonder my prayers used to be great medicine for me on sleepless nights.

God wants us to pray big, bold prayers. He wants us to offer prayers of significance that require Him to act. He wants our prayers to be ones no human can accomplish without His intervention. He wants us to rely on Him and He wants to answer our prayers of faith.

The Bible says,

"...The earnest prayer of a righteous person
has great power and produces wonderful results."

— James 5:16

If you do not write your prayers down, you will forget what you prayed about. When you forget, you do not see God responding to your prayers, so you repeatedly miss the blessings He provides.

WRITE THEM DOWN

Write them down! Word for word! Have a record of what you talked to God about. Go back a year from now and read your prayer journal and see if God is alive, and if He answered your prayers. See if He hears your prayers. See if He moves mountains and defeats the evil one. See how much He cares about you and what is important to you. See your life as part of His overall plan. "And we know that God causes everything to work together for the good of those who love God and are called according to His purpose for them," – Romans 8:28. Watch as He knits things together for good and for His purposes.

FUEL

If you want to fuel your personal relationship with The Lord, I believe there is nothing better than reading the Word slowly and writing out your prayers every day. *It is "FUEL to Ignite Your Soul."* It changed everything about my Spiritual life and about my relationship with Jesus. It changed the entire trajectory of my life.

You may recall from the beginning of this book how dismal my relationship was with Jesus. It was hollow, a shell, with nothing on the inside. I was embarrassed. I questioned my own salvation. Many times, I used prayer to put me asleep.

I am on a jet plane right now heading to Dubai and fuel makes this 14.5-hour, non-stop flight possible. The fuel worked at 45 degrees when we took off and the same fuel is working at -55 degrees right now. And it will work in the 80-degree temperatures when we land. The fuel turns the jet turbine and propels us 600 miles an hour at 39,000 feet, providing lights, heat, air, computers, food, and so on.

In the same way, Spiritual fuel works in all kinds of conditions and circumstances to light the fire within the soul. It keeps the fire in the soul burning. The fuel transforms our passive relationship with our Maker and catapults us to a daily, moment-by-moment, energized, interactive relationship with The Almighty. The fuel impacts our ability to see Him alive and active in our lives, which provides an even greater desire to know Him personally and to seek Him in our daily lives. This propels our relationship, surpassing our hopes and dreams of an intimacy with our Lord!

Fuel provides the energy to top a mountain, to cross a sea, to wander through the desert, and to survive an historically massive ice storm, snow storm, record cold temperatures or even the COVID-19 global pandemic.

This fuel also warms the heart, the soul, and provides comfort in any storm. It provides light on the darkest days and nights.

Today, my relationship with The Lord has *"done a complete 180."* Now I can hardly wait to read the Bible and pray. People call, text, and email, asking me to pray for them or their family and friends. I never cease to be amazed when I am asked to pray for someone. I often wonder, why me? It is, sometimes, overwhelming. It is like people think I have a direct connection to The Lord. Seriously! It is always very humbling.

I do not write these words because I am full of pride. In fact, writing this is difficult for me to do. I do not write it to say, "look at my prayer life," or "see how great my prayers are," or anything else to draw attention to myself. Rather, I write it to show you how far *God* has brought me on this journey. To show how my life has changed and how Jesus has changed me. How utilizing *The 40-Day Challenge* changed everything and how it can change your life, too. *The 40-Day Challenge* is the vehicle that gets you in a relationship with Jesus. *Jesus is the change agent.* He loves it when His Word and our prayer life changes us and our souls.

It is not about anything other than having a relationship with JESUS. That is the bottom line. Nothing else matters.

I believe your life with Jesus matters to you because you bought this book and you are still reading it. Several years ago, I was exactly where you may be today. It was hard to figure out. I was desperate and I think you might be too.

Micah was right. Something changed my life in 2009. I got serious about my relationship with Jesus.

"Your prayers will become the transcript of your life."
— Mark Batterson, Author,
Sr. Pastor, National Community Church, Washington, D.C.

If you will implement *The 40-Day Challenge,* you have my guarantee it will change your life or I will give you a complete refund (see page xi). What do you have to lose? It will not cost much money, nor take a lot of time. Trust me, it will change the trajectory of your life.

SECTION THREE
THE PREPARATION

CHAPTER 13

The Toolbox

You will need some specific things to make *The 40-Day Challenge* highly effective for you. I call it *The Toolbox*. You can pick these things up at any Mardel Christian & Education, or order online at mardel.com.

- A fresh Bible with wide margins
- A prayer journal
- Two different colored ink pens for your prayer journal
- A different pen especially made for Bibles that does not bleed through
- A pack of multi-colored highlighters made for use in a Bible

Just yesterday, I received an email from a complete stranger. He said, "I have problems reading the Bible and praying to God." He goes on to say, "I get embarrassed or uncomfortable. The better word is 'jealous' when I listen to them (his friends and wife) talk about God and what God has or is doing for them."

Reading his words, I knew those could have been mine 23 years ago. God used the words from a stranger to help motivate me to write this book. I am convinced my journey can help many overcome these issues. This book will help them to know they are not alone, and there is a cure for their pain. I needed to share my journey with others. You, too, can have a personal relationship with The LORD!

This book is not the law. You do not have to do it my way, but my way worked for me and a bunch of other people. I am certain that if you take *The 40-Day Challenge*, it will work for you, too.

I have prayed over this book since 2015. My prayer has been that, if I were honest about my early spiritual life and told my journey of how I overcame the embarrassment and frustrations of not knowing how to live in relationship to Jesus, it would bless the majority of readers and would give them hope and encouragement. Everyone would see it is possible. You can apply these simple truths and start having a heartfelt relationship with The Lord. So, may the use of this book set you free from guilt and shame or embarrassment and frustrations. May the formula I describe in these pages become the *"FUEL to Ignite Your Soul."*

Seek Him First

Can you imagine how fast your heart will be pumping when you see Jesus for the first time? Can you imagine spending eternity with Him?

No more pain, no more heartaches. No more Covid, no more funerals, no more politics, no more wars and no more deaths.

Just God The Father, Jesus The Son, The Holy Spirit, and the Angles along with the choosen spending eternity with The King of Kings. All of us in heaven perfectly designed for us from the beginning of time.

I can hardly wait. I love the words to the song "I Can Only Imagine" and to the song "Overwhelmed" and how about "He is Worthy!" I doubt I have accurately imagined what it will be like. I am sure I will be overwhelmed and I know I will be singing at the top of my lungs He is Worthy. What a day that will be.

It all started for me on my grandmother's front porch, sitting on her metal glider, during thunderstorms back in the '50's. She would hold me tight and tell me about God and his creation.

She planted the seeds of faith in my heart. Those germinated on August 3, 1970 in Springfield, Ohio at the First Christian Church. That night was my second birthday, my birth into the Kingdom of God. This was a defining moment in my life. This is my jubilee year as a follower of Jesus. A believer for 50 years and counting. I have tried to live for Him ever since; but as you have read, it (Please go to this link to see helpful photos: www. RossAlanHill.com/coin) has not always been easy or well done. I have shared how I drifted a good long while and faked my way through before I discovered how to have a personal, loving relationship with Jesus. Life has taught me, most of the time, I learn best while under duress.

You do not have to wonder how to have a relationship with Jesus ever again. You don't have to pretend or feel ashamed ever again. You can know Jesus and live in a genuine, personal, relationship with Jesus right now. He is available to all of us. The Lord makes promises, He never fails to keep them.

To find the *Fuel to Ignite Your Soul* start utilizing *The 40-Day Challenge*. I have personally guaranteed this book will change your relationship with Jesus. Now it is up to you, you are totally in control from here. It takes time and effort to form this new habit. Do it one day at a time. If you miss just pick it up tomorrow. No condemnation, just love and grace. God has promised it will happen and it will be worth the effort.

"Seek the Kingdom of God above all else, and live righteously, and he will give you everything you need."

— Matthew 6:33

Acknowledgments

It takes a team to write a book. I have a rock solid team to whom I am very appreciative. It starts with all of the people who have encouraged me to write this book. God used you to motivate me to do this work. There are so many of you, I could never begin to name you by name but you know if you are one of them and to you, I say, "thank you."

My wife R.J, who spent hours by herself so I could have the time to write this and then spent hours reading and re-reading it to help me get it right.

To my inner circle of friends who read the book and gave me valuable insights, suggestions and guidance and encouragement to write it. Ron Harris, Jim and Susan Stewart, Charbel and Christine Najem, Micah McGahan, and Matt Kutch. Your consistent encouragement helped me create this a tool.

To my prayer team who helped me write this book – Ron Harris, Matt Kutch Jim and Susan Stewart, and R.J. Hill – you carried a heavy load, thank you.

To all of my clients, friends and family that sent me countless stories of connecting with God, falling in love with God and constantly staying after me to write this book. Without your encouragement I would never have finished it. Thank you.

To my editors, Kathy and Matt Kutch, who are masterful editors and transformed my words, sentences and punctuation into literary excellence. Thank you both for your unselfish service and amazing patience to read and to re-read my transcript finding the errors and make the necessary adjustments.

To my friend and confidant Mark Batterson. A constant encourager and a terrific example. Thank you for your friendship and inspiration through the years. You are truly a blessing.

About the Author

Ross Alan Hill worked as a paper boy in grade school to buy baseball cards and in high school he worked in a sewage treatment plant to raise money to go to college. In college he worked as a guinea pig testing deodorant for Proctor and Gamble. As an adult, he built America's number one community bank based upon earnings in 2009 and number three in 2010. In retirement, he is building an executive coaching company and a non-profit organization to coach pastors.

After high school, with the help of his pastor, Hill enrolled in Cincinnati Bible Seminary. Hill says, "All of these life experiences instilled a strong work ethic, wisdom, faith, and a sense of humor. They also enhanced my critical thinking and problem-solving skills." Hill has successfully coached/mentored leaders for over three decades. His clients consist of some high impact and successful leaders, such as one of the 25 Most Powerful Women in Banking, a New York best-selling author, a world-class pediatric eye surgeon, the national head of a church denomination, and a two-time Olympic gold medal champion. Hill knows firsthand how difficult and lonely it can be at the top.

Hill is the author of *Broken Pieces: Nothing is Wasted*, an inspirational book designed to give hope and encouragement to everyone. Through a combination of real-life personal experiences and those of friends, customers, and acquaintances, he shares stories of truth learned over his life. Hill speaks about 40 times a year and is an executive coach, culture coach, and the Founder of Tall Oaks Coaching for pastors.

Notes

Notes

CPSIA information can be obtained
at www.ICGtesting.com
Printed in the USA
LVHW050716020921
696499LV00004B/13

9 780578 976051